IS STEM EVERYWHERE

IT'S ALIVE

THE SCIENCE OF BIOLOGY

JOHN LESLEY

REDBACK
publishing

Redback Publishing
PO Box 357 Frenchs Forest NSW 2086
Australia

www.redbackpublishing.com
orders@redbackpublishing.com

© Redback Publishing 2022

ISBN 978-1-925860-83-2

Author: John Lesley
Editor: Marlene Vaughan
Designer: Redback Publishing

Original illustrations © Redback Publishing 2022
Originated by Redback Publishing

Printed and bound in China

Acknowledgements
Abbreviations: l—left, r—right, b—bottom, t—top, c—centre, m—middle
We would like to thank the following for permission to reproduce photographs: (Images © shutterstock)

A catalogue record for this book is available from the National Library of Australia

CONTENTS

LIFE

Life is a rare occurrence. There certainly are billions of living things around you and even inside you right now, but the thin layer on the surface of our Earth seems to be the only place in our Solar System where life exists. Earth is the only place we know of at present with advanced life forms capable of exploring beyond their own planet.

There could be life further out in our Milky Way galaxy as well, but no-one knows for sure whether this is the case or not.

A person who studies the science of living things is called a biologist.

What has made Earth such a good place for life to appear, develop and spread across every habitable niche? Part of the answer involves the way life depends on genes for change and evolution. As life adapts to different habitats, it finds a better way to survive, resulting in more offspring being produced.

Whether the life form is a bacterium, a virus, a plant or a whale, we are all here now as a result of evolution. Adaptation to habitats, resulting from the forces of natural selection, has allowed the best adapted individuals to survive and transfer their genes to the next generation.

ALIVE, DEAD OR NON-LIVING

WHAT'S THE DIFFERENCE?

We can all look at a dead bird, a green plant or a rock and spot the one that is dead, alive or non-living. What are the characteristics of these things that allow us to put them into one of these three categories? By looking at the categories scientifically, we can more easily work out the boundaries between them.

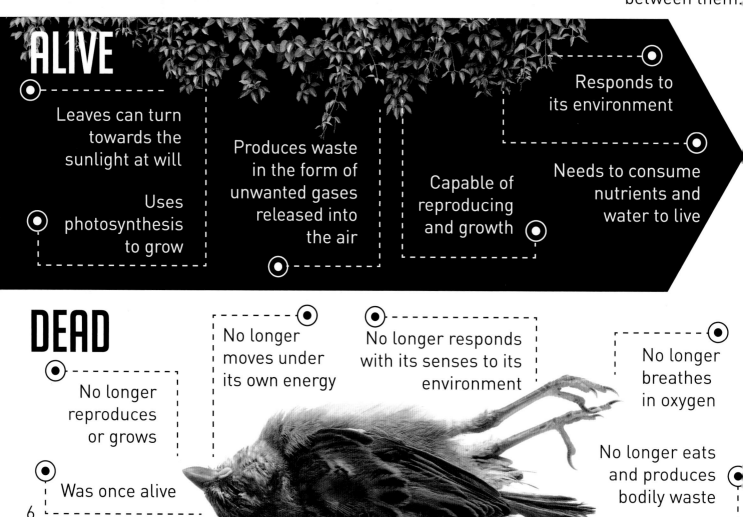

NON-LIVING

- Does not eat or produce waste
- Does not have sensory organs that allow it to respond to the environment
- Does not move using its own energy
- Does not breathe air
- Cannot actively reproduce itself

ALIVE

- Leaves can turn towards the sunlight at will
- Uses photosynthesis to grow
- Produces waste in the form of unwanted gases released into the air
- Capable of reproducing and growth
- Responds to its environment
- Needs to consume nutrients and water to live

DEAD

- No longer reproduces or grows
- Was once alive
- No longer moves under its own energy
- No longer responds with its senses to its environment
- No longer breathes in oxygen
- No longer eats and produces bodily waste

BASIC SIGNS OF LIFE

1 Consumes nutrients and produces waste

2 Moves using its own energy

3 Usually needs to use oxygen to survive

4 Grows using its own energy

5 Has organs that respond to conditions in the environment

6 Reproduces by producing offspring, or by making new cells that grow and heal its own injuries

Scientists who study the possibility of life beyond Earth are called exobiologists.

SEEDS

A hard seed can look like a stone. What makes the two different? By thinking about the characteristics of life, we can work out why a seed falls into the category of a living thing, while a stone does not.

Although most life on Earth needs oxygen to survive, there are a few microscopic creatures in the sea that use other gases to survive.

EXTRATERRESTRIAL LIFE

The list of points to look for when determining if something is living may be useful if we ever encounter life that is not from Earth. This sort of life could be completely different from what we are used to, and it may be difficult to work out if it is living or not just by looking at it.

EVOLUTION AND DNA

GIRAFFES HAVE
ADAPTED
TO SURVIVE

The millions of types of living things on Earth have all evolved.

Millions of years ago, an ancestor of a particular plant or animal changed slightly. If this change was beneficial, such as allowing them to better withstand heat or cold, then they lived a bit longer than others like themselves. This gave them time to produce more offspring with the same advantages. Over time, the continual process of change produced all the different types of plants and animals we know of today, as well as the ones that are extinct, like the dinosaurs.

HUMAN EVOLUTION

Human beings have evolved from ancient ancestors that were not at all like us today.

We have ancestors in common with all other animals. One of these ancestors was the first creature that was able to leave the oceans and live on land. This animal then evolved into all the land-living creatures.

After the first animals left the oceans to live on land, millions of years passed before the primate ancestors of humans evolved. Primate is a word that refers to apes, monkeys and humans. We are not descended from apes and monkeys alive now, but we do all have the same ancestors that lived a very long time ago.

DNA

Why does an elephant grow into an elephant, but a human grows into a human? It's because of their different DNA.

DNA is a chemical inside our cells. It is what genes are made of. Genes are where all the information is stored that tells our body to grow into us.

CELL

NUCLEUS

CHROMOSOME

DNA

GENE

NATURAL SELECTION

Natural selection occurs when a living thing acquires adaptations that make it able to survive better than others. It can then produce more offspring and may eventually evolve into a very different sort of living thing.

ANTIBIOTIC RESISTANT BACTERIA

Doctors are trying to reduce the amount of antibiotics they give patients. This is because natural selection allows drug resistant bacteria to live and multiply. The infection then stops responding to antibiotics and the patient may become very sick.

ANTIBIOTICS KILL THE BAD BACTERIA

SOME BACTERIA ARE DRUG RESISTANT

DRUG RESISTANT BACTERIA LIVE AND MULTIPLY

WE'RE ALL MADE OF CELLS

All living things are made of tiny parts called cells. Bacteria have only one cell, but humans have billions. If you look at your skin through a microscope, you will see that it is a mass of tiny cells all joined together.

CELLS AT WORK

Blood cells develop a red colour and don't join together but race around separately in our blood

Plant cells develop into leaves, flowers and roots

Bone cells make bone

MAIN PARTS OF A PLANT CELL

CYTOPLASM WATERY INTERIOR OF THE CELL

NUCLEUS - PART INSIDE THE CELL THAT SEPARATES AND STORES THE GENES AND DNA

CELL WALL

CELL MEMBRANE

ANIMAL CELLS

Animal cells have a cell membrane, but they do not have cell walls or green chlorophyll.

Human skin cells contain a pigment called melanin. This gives skin its different colours.

ANIMAL CELL

PLANT CELLS

Plant cells have a cell wall that is strong enough to allow the plant to stand up. Green plant cells contain a chemical called chlorophyll. Plants use this in photosynthesis to grow.

PLANT CELL

BACTERIA

Bacteria have a cell membrane, like animals, but they do not have a separate nucleus to store their genes and DNA.

11

PUTTING LIFE INTO GROUPS

There are billions of living things on Earth. Scientists divide them all into groups in a process called classification.

CLASSIFICATION

THE MAIN GROUPS OF LIVING THINGS

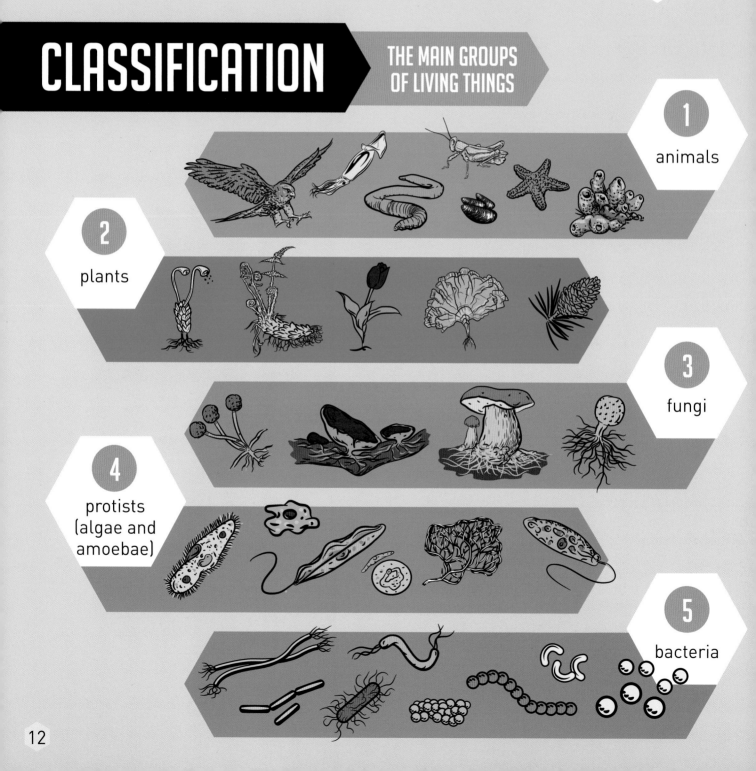

1 animals

2 plants

3 fungi

4 protists (algae and amoebae)

5 bacteria

VIRUSES

Viruses cause colds and COVID-19 in people. A different sort of virus infection causes yellow markings on green leaves.

Viruses are an unusual type of life. They can stay in a semi-living condition for a very long time, waiting for the chance to infect the cell of a living creature. Only then can they start to grow and reproduce.

ANIMALS

The group of all animals is called the **animal kingdom**.

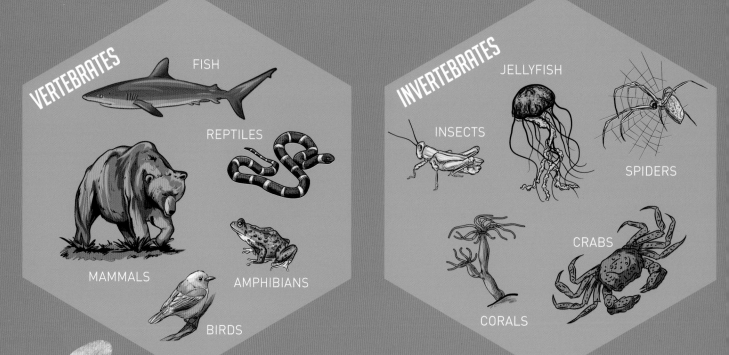

VERTEBRATES

FISH

REPTILES

MAMMALS

AMPHIBIANS

BIRDS

INVERTEBRATES

JELLYFISH

INSECTS

SPIDERS

CRABS

CORALS

MAMMALS

All mammals feed their young on milk, are warm-blooded and have fur or hair.

MARSUPIALS
Give birth to underdeveloped babies
- **kangaroo**
- **possum**
- **koala**

PLACENTALS
Give birth to well developed babies
- **human**
- **dog**
- **dolphin**

MONOTREMES
Lay eggs
- **echidna**
- **platypus**

PLANTS

THE MAIN PARTS OF VASCULAR PLANTS

(A vascular plant is one which has special cells that carry fluids from the roots to the stems and leaves.)

The group of all plants is called the **plant kingdom**

LEAVES

Photosynthesis in green leaves combines water, light and carbon dioxide to produce the sugars that plants need for growth.

STEMS

Stems hold the plant up and contain cells that transfer water and nutrients from the roots below the ground to the leaves and flowers at the top.

ROOTS

Roots anchor the plant in the soil and they absorb nutrients and water.

NON-FLOWERING PLANTS

Reproduce by creating winged seeds that are released from cones
- **fir trees**
- **cyprusses**
- **redwoods**

FLOWERING PLANTS

Produce flowers and seeds

- **roses**
- **wheat**
- **bottlebrush**
- **daisies**
- **grass**

MOSSES AND FERNS

Reproduce by releasing spores into the air
- **asparagus fern**
- **maidenhair fern**

LIFE NEEDS FOOD

All living things need food and water to survive, grow and reproduce.

WHAT IS FOOD?

We often eat without thinking about why we are eating, or about what the food we are putting in our mouths is made from.

JUNK FOOD

If we eat junk food with few nutritious chemicals in it, we may end up lacking the vitamins and minerals we require to keep our bodies working well. We may also not grow properly.

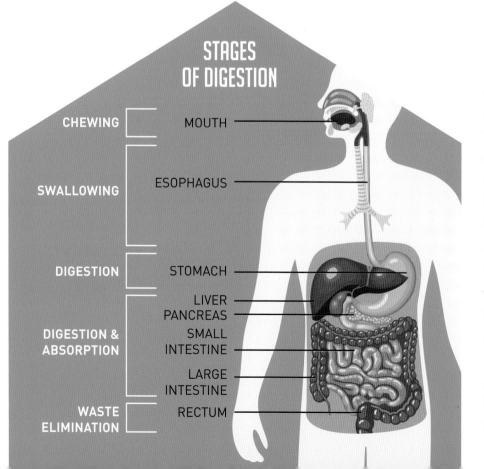

STAGES OF DIGESTION

CHEWING	MOUTH
SWALLOWING	ESOPHAGUS
DIGESTION	STOMACH
DIGESTION & ABSORPTION	LIVER PANCREAS SMALL INTESTINE LARGE INTESTINE
WASTE ELIMINATION	RECTUM

Food is made from chemicals. As we chew and swallow it, our body starts to break it down into the chemicals we need to live. A piece of birthday cake or a lettuce leaf all get broken down in our stomach and intestines in a process called digestion. The chemicals then pass into our blood and are carried around our bodies to where they are needed for growth or the repair of injuries.

Animals get rid of the waste from their food by producing faeces and urine.

HOW DO PLANTS EAT?

Roots absorb nutrients from the soil and spread them to cells in every part of the plant.

PHOTOSYNTHESIS

SUNLIGHT

CARBON DIOXIDE

SUGAR

OXYGEN

WATER

Plants are special because they create their own energy in the form of sugar. They do this through a chemical process called photosynthesis, which needs the green chlorophyll that is in leaves.

FINDING FOOD MEANS LIFE OR DEATH

The availability of food is one of the major factors that determine where living things can exist.

A lion cannot exist in the ocean because it does not have the adaptations to live and hunt there. For the same reasons, a dolphin cannot exist on the grasslands of Africa. Each of these animals has adaptations that allow it to use the food sources in its own habitat.

Plants will not grow if they are in soil that has no water or nutrients that they can absorb. A cactus can grow in a hot desert because it can store water, but a rainforest tree would die in the same environment because it has evolved to need access to a lot of water in the soil.

TAKE A BIG BREATH

We breathe because we need the oxygen in the air to survive. Without oxygen, nearly all life on Earth would die.

WHAT IS THAT AIR YOU JUST BREATHED IN DOING INSIDE YOU?

From our lungs, the oxygen passes into our blood and is carried around our body. Inside cells, the oxygen is used to help make the energy we need to live and grow. In this chemical process, carbon dioxide is released. It passes into the blood and when it reaches the lungs we breathe it out. Carbon dioxide is one of our waste products.

There are a few tiny organisms that live in water and do not seem to need oxygen to live.

OXYGEN

The air we breathe contains about 21% oxygen gas.

CARBON DIOXIDE

DIAPHRAGM

DIAPHRAGM

Living things use oxygen and release carbon dioxide, but not all of them have lungs to do this. Microscopic animals, such as bacteria, just pass the gases back and forth across their cell membranes.

Fish have gills instead of lungs. Oxygen passes from the water into their blood across the thin surface of the gills. A very hot day can heat up the water in a shallow lake or a fish tank. This causes the oxygen in the water to disappear into the air. Fish then struggle to survive.

DO PLANTS BREATHE?

Yes! Plants need oxygen too. At night, when there is no sunlight, plants cannot make their own energy using photosynthesis. In the dark, plant cells use oxygen in the air, and release carbon dioxide, just like we do all the time. Once the Sun comes out, plants start using carbon dioxide and releasing oxygen into the air.

Animals breathe the oxygen that plants release. Animal life could not have evolved on Earth if plants had not made the air just right for us by adding lots of oxygen to it.

REPRODUCTION

LIVING THINGS ALL REPRODUCE THEMSELVES. THIS IS ONE OF THE CHARACTERISTICS OF LIFE.

There are two main ways that life produces a new generation:

1 Organisms whose bodies consist of one cell reproduce by just dividing into two cells. Bacteria do this. All the new bacteria are the same as each other.

2 Multicellular organisms usually reproduce sexually. This means there is a male and a female individual and each contributes genetic information to the offspring. This is the way that humans reproduce. Since both parents are needed to create the offspring, children look like both their parents, but are not exactly the same as either of them.

Sexual reproduction allows a mixing of genetic information that is beneficial to survival. Since the offspring are not exactly the same as the parents, the new generation is likely to have differences that may be useful if the environment or habitat changes.

HOW PLANTS REPRODUCE

Flowering plants produce seeds that can grow into new plants.

Plants reproduce sexually. Flowers have a male part, called the stamen, which produces pollen. The pollen gets dusted onto the female part when it is carried there by insects or blown there by the wind. This process is called pollination.

When bees collect pollen from flowers, they are helping the flower to create seeds by spreading the pollen around. Without bees, many of the plants we rely on for food would not be able to produce seeds and grow new plants.

POLLINATOR

POLLEN

POLLEN

POLLEN

POLLEN GRAINS ON STAMEN

SEED

Humans eat seeds, the new plants that grow from them, and the fruit that forms as well. Wheat is a seed and so are nuts.

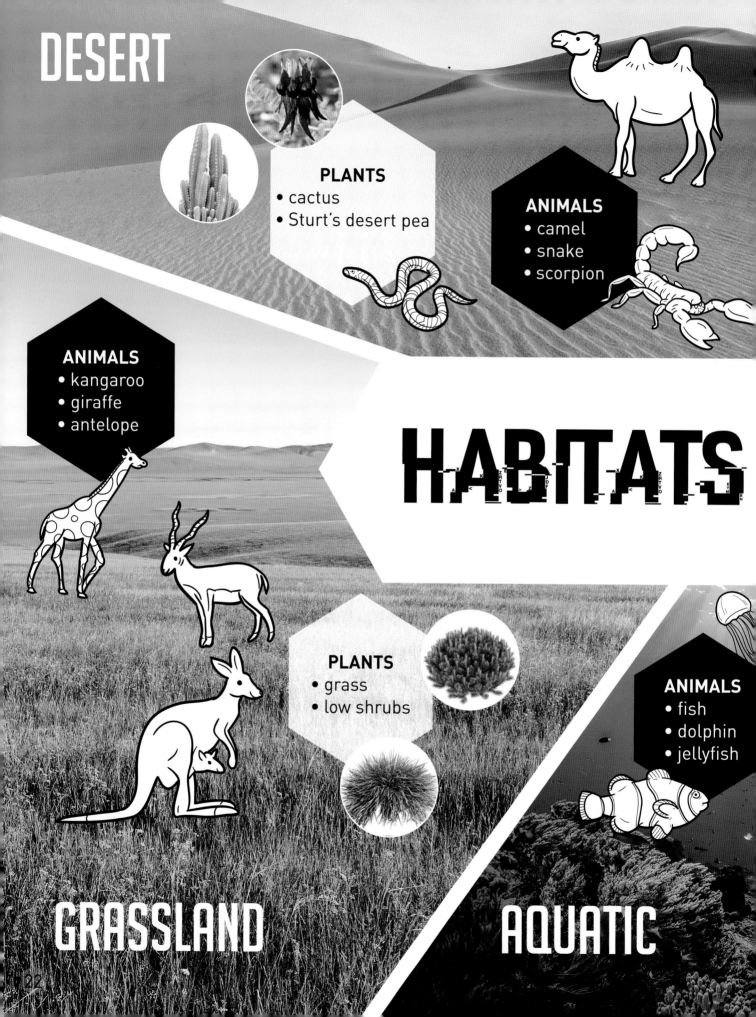

DESERT

PLANTS
- cactus
- Sturt's desert pea

ANIMALS
- camel
- snake
- scorpion

ANIMALS
- kangaroo
- giraffe
- antelope

HABITATS

PLANTS
- grass
- low shrubs

ANIMALS
- fish
- dolphin
- jellyfish

GRASSLAND

AQUATIC

22

FOREST

ANIMALS
- panda
- orangutan
- koala

PLANTS
- pine tree
- rubber
- tree fern

AND HOMES

ANIMALS
- penguin
- polar bear
- sea lion

PLANTS
- seagrass
- kelp
- algae

PLANTS
- lichen
- moss

SNOW AND ICE

ADAPTING TO CHANGE

Animals that live in the snow are the result of thousands and even millions of years of evolution. Over time, lots of little changes eventually result in an adaptation that makes the animal better at surviving than its ancestors were in the long distant past.

Living things survive in vastly different environments because they have developed adaptations.

An adaptation is a change in body structure or behaviour that enables a living thing to survive in conditions that might be disastrous for another life form that does not have the same adaptations.

Penguins have adapted their wings to help them swim through the water.

An adaptation does not happen immediately. If you were suddenly placed in a snow-covered environment without any way to keep warm, you would probably not survive.

Mountain hares turn white in winter for camouflage

ADAPTING BY CHANGING BEHAVIOUR

MIGRATION

Making the best use of the environment does not always mean staying in the one place. Some animals have developed a behaviour called migration. Many animals, including insects, birds, land mammals, whales, turtles and fish all move from one area to another, often over thousands of kilometres.

REASONS FOR ANIMAL MIGRATION

Finding a safe place to breed

Finding a climate that is not too hot or too cold

Going to places where food is more abundant

HIBERNATION

Rather than going on a long journey to escape a cold winter, some animals hibernate. They sleep through the cold weather and only wake up when spring comes. Hibernation is a very special type of sleeping. The animal's body functions all slow down, so it uses very little energy and does not need to eat or drink. The heart rate slows and the body temperature falls.

Sometimes the hibernation is timed to end at exactly the same time as a plentiful food supply becomes available. In Australia, the eastern pigmy possum hibernates through the icy winter on snow-covered mountains. It wakes up just as the Bogong moths appear, providing the possums with a nutritious source of food.

ANIMALS THAT HIBERNATE
• Polar bears • Grizzly bears • Hamsters
• Echidnas • Eastern pygmy possums

MOVING AROUND

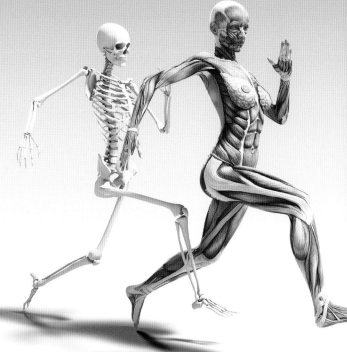

ANIMALS

One of the ways we determine if something is alive is if it moves by itself. We move by using our muscles to make our skeleton move. This movement needs energy that comes from our food.

Intelligent animals, such as humans, also move around because they are curious. Humans have moved as far away as the Moon because they want to know what is there.

CORALS

It is easy to see how large animals move, but what about little creatures such as corals? Coral does not seem to move. It looks very much like a rock. Actually, the living parts of coral do move all the time. They sweep food into their mouths and the baby corals swim around in the water until they find somewhere to settle down and grow.

WHY DO ANIMALS MOVE AROUND SO MUCH?

to find food and water

to find a mate

to find shelter

to escape danger

26

PLANTS MOVE TOO

Look at a plant in the soil. It cannot move from where its roots are anchored, but parts of the plant do move.

Roots in the ground start growing in the direction of water

Some sex cells of plants move so that they can join together to make seeds

A Venus flytrap plant snaps its trap shut very quickly to catch insects

Leaves and flowers bend towards the sunlight

27

FOOD CHAINS

All life on Earth is connected, sometimes in ways that we do not realise.

Food chains are one of the ways that life is interconnected. Plants that make sugar from sunlight are the basis of the existence of life. Even those animals that are meat eaters, like lions and tigers, depend on plants, since they eat animals that are herbivores (plant eaters).

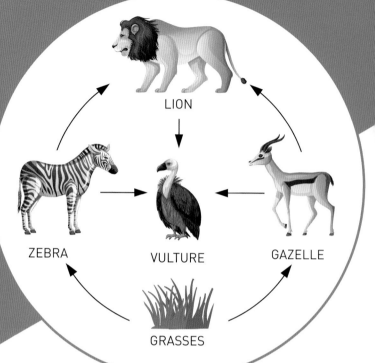

LION

ZEBRA

VULTURE

GAZELLE

GRASSES

In the oceans, sharks eat fish that, in turn, have eaten smaller creatures. At some point along the chain, an animal has eaten tiny living things called plankton.

DESTROYING A FOOD CHAIN

Some food chains are very complex. Pollution that destroys one part of the food chain can result in animals further up the chain reducing in numbers.

Sometimes we do not realise the reason for a decline in animal numbers until we trace the food chain back to a point where pollution caused by humans has affected one particular animal. Poisons from rubbish in the oceans are absorbed by fish, which are then eaten by larger predators. These large animals may then become sick, stop reproducing or even die.

SENSES AND COMMUNICATING

Living things have senses that allow them to react to what is happening around them. Humans have 5 basic senses:

SIGHT
HEARING
SMELL
TASTE
TOUCH

One of the ways that life uses its senses is to communicate with other living things. Animals and plants communicate with each other, as well as with other individuals in their own species.

A species is a separate type of living thing

Plants release perfumes to attract bees to the flowers. They also attract animals to ripe fruit with smell and colour. The animals then eat the fruit and help to spread the seeds in their droppings.

UNUSUAL SENSES

Bees can see ultraviolet light. If we illuminate flowers with ultraviolet light, they reveal patterns on them that are normally invisible to us.

Pigeons and other birds that migrate over very long distances may be able to sense the Earth's magnetic field.

A platypus uses its bill to sense the weak electric currents created by other creatures in the water.

Some snakes can see the heat around an animal, making them deadly hunters even in the dark.

WORDS ABOUT BIOLOGY

bacteria single celled organisms that do not have a cell nucleus

carnivore meat eater

chlorophyll green pigment that allows plants to photosynthesise

cytoplasm watery interior of a cell

DNA chemicals that make up genes in cells

exobiologist person who studies the possibility of life beyond Earth

extraterrestrial beyond the Earth

gene parts of a cell that control the way a living thing grows

herbivore plant eater

invertebrate animal without a backbone

mammal type of animal that feeds its young on milk and is covered in hair or fur

marsupial type of mammal that produces underdeveloped young that usually then grow in a pouch on the outside of the mother

melanin brown pigment in animal skin and hair

monotreme type of mammal that lays eggs

niche special place where a living thing can survive

nucleus (cell) separate part storing the genes inside a cell

photosynthesis process plants use to convert sunlight into food

placental type of mammal that produces live, well developed young

primates animals including humans, apes and monkeys

ultraviolet light light with a short wavelength and damaging effects on living cells

vascular plants plants with special cells for transporting water from roots to stems and flowers

vertebrate animal with a backbone

virus life form that can only grow by infecting the cell of another living thing

INDEX